THE GEARHEAD'S GUIDE TO
GO-KARTS

BY LISA J. AMSTUTZ

CAPSTONE PRESS
a capstone imprint

Published by Spark, an imprint of Capstone
1710 Roe Crest Drive, North Mankato, Minnesota 56003
capstonepub.com

Library of Congress Cataloging-in-Publication Data is available on the Library of Congress website.
ISBN: 9781666356441 (hardcover)
ISBN: 9781666356458 (ebook PDF)

Summary: Go-karts are fun and fast. These small vehicles can be made even stronger and faster, and readers will love finding out how! Full of action-packed photos and accessible text, this high-interest book puts the reader behind the wheel.

Editorial Credits
Editor: Erika L. Shores; Designer: Heidi Thompson; Media Researchers: Jo Miller and Pam Mitsakos; Production Specialist: Tori Abraham

Image Credits
Alamy: Jason Jones, 5, Jules Glazier, 23; Getty Images: fotogaby, 21, microgen, 25, romaset, 12; Shutterstock: A.PAES, 6, Aaron of L.A. Photography, 4, Babyboom, 20, Hiram Gil Solano, 15, i3alda, throughout, design element, Jibjeep_Photo, 24, Margo Harrison, 26-27, PhotoStock10, 29, ROMAN DZIUBALO, Cover, Surasak_Photo, 7, 9, 17, 19, TACHEFOTO, 13, Weblogiq, 28, Yaresik, 11

Capstone thanks Kevin Dick, technology education instructor in Mankato, MN, for his assistance in reviewing this book.

Table of Contents

Words in **bold** are in the glossary.

Small Speedsters

Start your engines! Go-karts come in many shapes and sizes. You can race them or ride them off-road. These small cars are fun to tinker with. Try a few of these mods to make your kart even cooler!

FACT

Many race car drivers got their start with go-karts. There are two types of kart races. Sprints are short. Enduro races are long.

Built for Speed

Does your kart need more speed?
Try a new engine. Pick one with more
horsepower. It will help you **accelerate**
faster. It will reach a higher top speed.

Two-stroke engines are light and speedy. Four-stroke engines are good for long races. They use less fuel.

cylinder head of four-stroke engine

You can also re-gear your kart for top speed. Put a smaller **sprocket** on the rear axle. Or choose one without as many teeth. Don't go too small though. The engine might put too much force on the axle. This could harm your go-kart.

Maybe you want to speed up faster. If so, then use a larger sprocket on the rear axle.

sprocket

axle

Less weight means more speed.

Look at each part of your go-kart.

See if you can swap it for a lighter one.

Try a new frame, seat, and bumpers.

Or swap out your pedals and fuel tank.

Take off extra seats or other parts you

do not need.

FACT

Art Ingels built the first go-kart in 1956.
He used a lawnmower motor and some
metal tubing. He called it a "little car."

Which tires are right for you? It depends on your **terrain**. Racing karts use smooth tires. These are called slicks. They have no **tread**. Their soft rubber grips the track. Off-road tires have deep tread. These knobby tires can handle mud or dirt.

Many drivers use larger back tires on their karts. They use smaller ones in front. Large tires give more traction. Small ones make it easier to steer.

Power Boost

Tune up your **carburetor** for a power boost. Turn the screw clockwise to adjust it. This will let in more fuel and air. Swap the **stock** jet for a bigger one. This will let more fuel in too.

FACT

Some go-karts run on gas. Others are electric. Some just use pedal power!

carburetor

Still need more power? Swap out your stock **exhaust** system. Try a high-flow header instead. You will also want a new air filter. It will let more air reach the fuel.

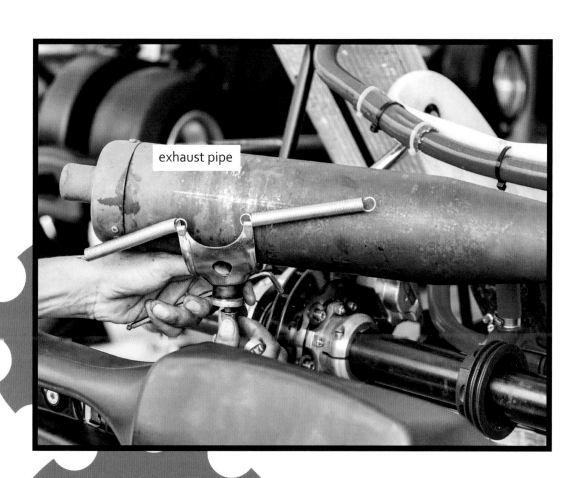

exhaust pipe

Look for other ways to boost your kart's speed and power. Adjust the speed limiter on your engine. Then your kart can reach higher speeds.

engine

You can also add a **nitrous oxide** kit. It adds oxygen. Then more fuel can be burned. More fuel means more power.

Cool Karts

Riding your kart off-road? Trail riders will want a roll cage. This frame of steel bars goes over the top of the go-kart. It helps protect drivers in a crash.

FACT

Go-kart drivers need safety gear. A helmet and chest protector keep drivers safe in a crash. Gloves and a suit prevent scrapes and burns.

A bouncy ride can be hard on your arms. Try a steering wheel with a foam grip. The foam will help absorb shocks.

Not all steering wheels are round.

You may prefer a butterfly shape.

It takes up less space in the kart.

Need a new look? Paint your kart to make it stand out on the track. Try a dragon or tiger design. Or add flames and racing stripes.

Add **decals** to your kart. Make your own or buy them at a store. You can make stickers with your team name.

Safety gear doesn't have to be boring. Pick a colorful suit and gloves. Add patches. Or stick decals on your helmet. Show off your team in style.

Try a few of these hacks. Or come up with some of your own. Now you're ready to race!

Glossary

accelerate (ak-SEL-uh-rayt)—to increase the speed of something

carburetor (KAHR-buh-ray-tuhr)—a part of the engine that mixes oxygen with fuel before it is forced into the engine cylinders

decal (DEE-kal)—a design printed on a sticker

exhaust (eg-ZAWST)—the pipes that carry gases away from an engine

horsepower (HORS-pou-ur)—a unit for measuring an engine's power

nitrous oxide (NEYE-truhss OK-side)—a gas made up of nitrogen and oxygen

sprocket (SPROK-it)—a wheel with a rim of toothlike points that fit into the holes of a chain

stock (STOK)—the parts of a vehicle installed by the factory

terrain (tuh-RAYN)—land or ground

tread (TRED)—a series of bumps and deep grooves on a tire

Read More

Adamson, Thomas K. *Karts*. Minneapolis: Bellwether Media, 2019.

Gish, Ashley. *Karts*. Mankato, MN: Creative Education, 2021.

Katirgis, Jane, and Alison G. Norville. *Racing Karts*. New York: Enslow Publishing, 2018.

Internet Sites

American Kart Racing Association
akraracing.com/

Kartbuilding
kartbuilding.net

World Karting Association
worldkarting.com/

Index

About the Author

Lisa J. Amstutz is the author of more than 150 books for children. She enjoys reading and writing about science and technology. Lisa lives on a small farm in Ohio with her family.